# THIS BOOK BELONGS TO:

__________________________

Made in the USA
Columbia, SC
18 December 2024

49721624R00061